Fact Finders®

The
Solar System
and Beyond

The Milky Way and Other Galaxies

by Megan Kopp

Consultant:
Dr. Ilia I. Roussev
Associate Astronomer
Institute for Astronomy
University of Hawaii at Manoa

CAPSTONE PRESS
a capstone imprint

Fact Finders are published by Capstone Press,
151 Good Counsel Drive, P.O. Box 669, Mankato, Minnesota 56002.
www.capstonepub.com

 Books published by Capstone Press are manufactured with paper
containing at least 10 percent post-consumer waste.

Library of Congress Cataloging-in-Publication Data
Kopp, Megan.
 The Milky Way and other galaxies / by Megan Kopp.
 p. cm.—(Fact finders. The solar system and beyond)
 Summary: "Describes the Milky Way and other galaxies, including what they're made of, shapes, and
clusters"—Provided by publisher.
 Includes bibliographical references and index.
 ISBN 978-1-4296-6002-0 (lib. bdg.)
 ISBN 978-1-4296-7227-6 (pbk.)
 1. Milky Way—Juvenile literature. 2. Galaxies—Juvenile literature. I. Title. II. Series.
 QB857.7.K664 2012
 523.1'13—dc22   2010052354

Editorial Credits
Jennifer Besel, editor; Heidi Thompson, designer; Eric Manske, production specialist

Photo Credits
Alamy: Galaxy Picture Library/Peter Shah, 17; Getty Images Inc.: Time Life Pictures/Jon Brenneis, 5;
NASA, 22, 23; NASA, ESA, and A. Feild (STScI), 13; NASA, ESA, and A. Nota (STScI/ESA), 19; NASA,
ESA, and STScI, 9; NASA, ESA, and the Hubble Heritage (STScI/AURA)-ESA/Hubble Collaboration,
9, 18; NASA, ESA, and the Hubble Heritage Team (STScI/AURA), 3, 9, 29; NASA, ESA, M.J. Jee and H.
Ford (John Hopkins University), 10; NASA/JPL-Caltech, 15, 21; NASA/JPL-Caltech/R. Hurt (SSC), 25;
NASA/JSC, 27; Photo Researchers, Inc/Mark Garlick, 7, 20; Shutterstock/Konstantin Mironov, 5; The
Hubble Heritage Team (AURA/STScI/NASA), cover, 1

Artistic Effects
iStockphoto: Dar Yang Yan, Nickilford

Printed in the United States of America in Stevens Point, Wisconsin.
092010   005934WZS11

Table of Contents

Chapter 1

Discovering Galaxies

The ancient Greeks studied the night sky more than 2,000 years ago. They saw what looked liked clouds. They called the clouds the "milky way" because they looked like a stream of milk.

Fast forward to the early 1600s and the invention of the telescope. Telescopes made space objects brighter and easier to see. As telescopes got bigger and better, scientists could see even more. They discovered that the Milky Way isn't a cloud. It is actually billions of stars grouped together. They called this collection of stars a galaxy.

In the early 1920s, Edwin Hubble made a discovery. He found a group of stars that was too far away to be part of the Milky Way. This star group had to be a separate galaxy. Hubble went on to discover billions of galaxies. Each galaxy was made up of billions of stars. The universe suddenly became bigger than anyone had imagined.

Edwin Hubble

the Milky Way as
seen from Earth

Forming the Universe

Scientists have puzzled over how the universe formed for years. Most agree on a basic theory. They believe the universe started forming about 14 billion years ago. All the matter in the universe was packed into a space smaller than a grain of sand. The space was hot and crowded. One day the space exploded and blew outward. Astronomers call this explosion idea the big bang theory.

About half a billion years after the big bang, scientists think dust clouds began grouping together. The building blocks for forming galaxies were in place.

But scientists don't agree on what happened next. Some think that clusters of about 1 million stars formed first. Later the clusters gathered into galaxies. Other scientists believe that clouds of gases and dust began spinning around a central point. These gas and dust clouds formed disc shapes. After these discs formed, stars began to form.

300,000 yrs

the big bang

theory: an idea that explains something that is unknown

matter: anything that has weight and takes up space

Formation of the Universe

13.7 billion yrs

9 billion yrs

300 million yrs

dust clouds
begin to form

stars and galaxies
begin to form

atoms begin
to form

the universe today

Chapter 2

Understanding Galaxies

All galaxies are made of stars, gas, and dust. These ingredients are held together by gravity. Gravity pulls stars, gases, and dust in orbit around a galaxy's center.

Galaxies are not all alike, though. They vary in size and in the number of stars they contain. They also have different shapes. Galaxies are either elliptical, spiral, or irregular.

Elliptical galaxies are the most common type. These galaxies look like flattened globes. Elliptical galaxies are filled with stars. They have very little gas or dust. Almost all the stars in elliptical galaxies are very old.

Spiral galaxies have a bright center. Flat arms of stars, gas, and dust wrap around the middle. Barred spiral galaxies have a line of stars across the center.

gravity: a force that pulls objects together

orbit: the path an object follows as it goes around a galaxy

Spiral galaxies make one or two new stars each year.

spiral galaxy

irregular galaxy

elliptical galaxy

Irregular galaxies don't have a set shape. They look more like clouds. Why do some galaxies have a loose cloud shape and others have a definite shape? That's one of the mysteries of space yet to be solved.

FACT: Scientists don't know what dark matter is made of or how it works. They just know it exists.

Scientists think the black areas in this galaxy cluster are dark matter.

Dark Matter

Scientists have also discovered that galaxies are made of things that can't be seen. One of these invisible pieces is called dark matter.

The discovery of dark matter started with a mystery. Scientists knew that gravity pulls stars around a galaxy's center. They also knew that the less **mass** an area has, the weaker the pull of gravity. Galaxies have fewer stars on their outer edges. So scientists reasoned that the outer stars orbit slower because gravity's pull would be weaker. The trouble was, the outer stars weren't slower. Scientists realized there must be more matter in the outer edges of galaxies than they could see.

Dark matter is an invisible material. But if scientists can't see it, how can they prove it's there? Matter is a term used for any kind of stuff that has mass. And anything with mass has a gravitational pull on other objects. Scientists know dark matter exists because they have seen the effects of its gravity on other objects.

mass: the amount of material in an object

Dark Energy

Galaxies contain another invisible force called dark energy. But it took a long time for scientists to figure out how dark energy worked.

Every bit of matter in the universe is pulling on other bits of matter. With all this pulling, scientists expected the universe would be shrinking. But in 1929, Edwin Hubble discovered just the opposite. The universe is expanding!

How is that possible? Scientists realized there must be an invisible energy within galaxies. This dark energy is causing the universe to expand. But they couldn't prove it existed.

In 2010 scientists finally found a way to measure dark energy. Using the Hubble Space Telescope, scientists looked through a cluster of galaxies. This cluster magnified the light coming from galaxies beyond it. The scientists measured how light from the distant galaxies bends as it travels through the telescope's lens. They could measure how dark energy pushed matter apart.

magnify: to make something look larger than it really is

Cosmic Tug of War

The force of dark energy becomes greater than that of dark matter as time goes on.

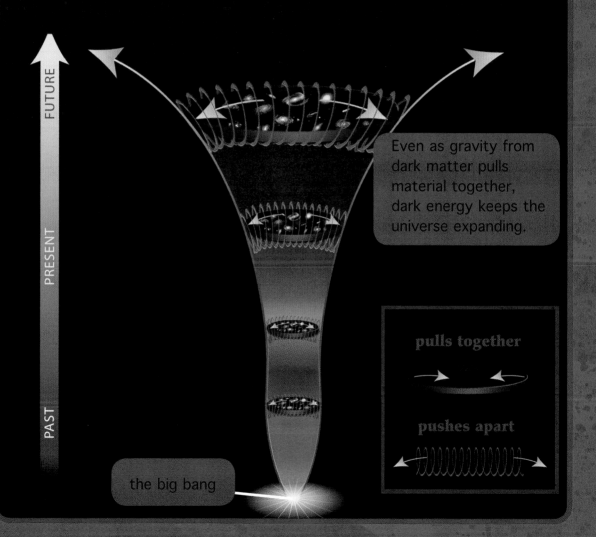

FUTURE

PRESENT

PAST

Even as gravity from dark matter pulls material together, dark energy keeps the universe expanding.

pulls together

pushes apart

the big bang

Chapter 3

Galaxy Tours

The cloudy band of light in the sky is only a small part of our home galaxy. Galaxies are so big that scientists use the speed of light to measure them. The Milky Way is 100,000 light-years across. It's about 10,000 light-years thick.

The Milky Way is so big, humans have not yet been able to leave it. But if we could look at the Milky Way from above, it would look like a big pinwheel. It has a center core with a thick bar of stars. Spiraling arms of gas, dust, and stars curve off the center bar. Scientists call the Milky Way a barred spiral galaxy.

Our solar system is located in the spiral arm Orion. The Sun orbits the center of the Milky Way. It speeds around the galaxy at 563,000 miles (906,000 kilometers) per hour. Even at this rate, it takes 220 million years to go all the way around the galaxy.

light-year: a unit used to measure distance in space; 1 light-year equals about 6 trillion miles (9.5 trillion km)

The Milky Way

The Milky Way

FACT: Our solar system is about 24,000 light-years away from the center of the Milky Way.

bar of stars

core

Sun

Orion arm

The Milky Way is not alone in the universe. Astronomers believe there are more than 100 billion galaxies. Of these, only three can be seen from Earth without a telescope. These three are Andromeda and the Small and Large Magellanic Clouds.

Andromeda

People in the Northern Hemisphere can see the spiral galaxy Andromeda. This galaxy is 250,000 light-years across. Because of its size, Andromeda is the most distant object we can see without a telescope.

Scientists study Andromeda to learn about our own spiral galaxy. In fact, some call it the Milky Way's big sister. Astronomers have discovered close to 300 star clusters in Andromeda. But Andromeda is about 2.3 million light-years from the Milky Way. Not much else is known about the stars there or any possible planets.

Galaxies orbit the universe. Sometimes they crash into each other and form a single galaxy. That's what scientists think will happen with Andromeda and the Milky Way. The galaxies are traveling toward each other at about 300,000 miles (483,000 km) per hour. But scientists don't expect a crash to happen for 3 billion years.

Large and Small Magellanic Clouds

The Large and Small Magellanic Clouds are galaxies that orbit the Milky Way. Both Magellanic Clouds are irregular-shaped, dwarf galaxies.

The Large Magellanic Cloud is 170,000 light-years away. Doradus is one of the brightest stars in the Large Magellanic Cloud.

dwarf galaxy: a small galaxy with only a few billion stars

a star forming region in the Large Magellanic Cloud

FACT:

The Small Magellanic Cloud has only a few billion stars. It is actually being pulled apart by the Milky Way's gravity. Eventually all the matter in the Small Magellanic Cloud will become part of the Milky Way. Of course, this won't happen in our lifetimes. The Small Magellanic Cloud is still 210,000 light-years away.

stars being born in the Small Magellanic Cloud

Galaxy Clusters

Galaxies are often drawn together by gravity to form clusters. The Milky Way is part of a cluster known as the Local Group. The Local Group is about 10 million light-years across. The largest galaxies in the Local Group are the Milky Way, Andromeda, and Triangulum. The cluster also includes about 40 dwarf galaxies. Some galaxy clusters contain thousands of galaxies.

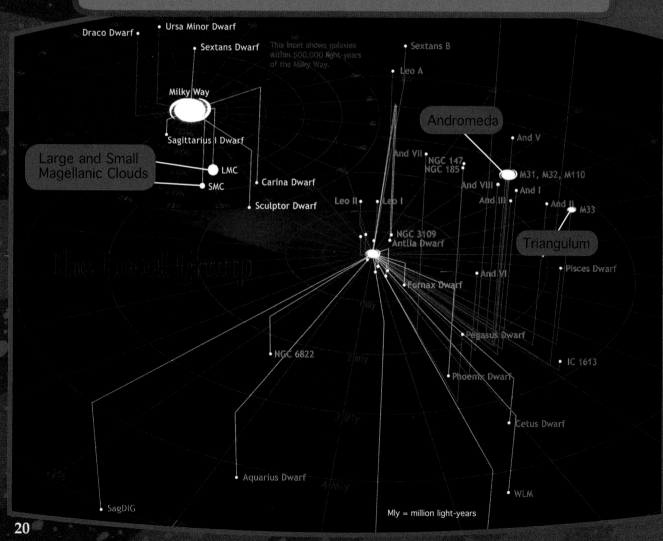

Draco Dwarf •   • Ursa Minor Dwarf   • Sextans B

• Sextans Dwarf   This inset shows galaxies within 500,000 light-years of the Milky Way.

• Leo A

Milky Way

Andromeda   • And V

• Sagittarius I Dwarf

And VII •   NGC 147   NGC 185 •

Large and Small Magellanic Clouds

• LMC   • Carina Dwarf

• SMC

And VIII •   • M31, M32, M110   • And I

• Sculptor Dwarf   Leo II •   • Leo I   And III •   • And II   M33

NGC 3109   Antlia Dwarf

Triangulum

The Local Group

• Pisces Dwarf

• And VI

• Fornax Dwarf

• Pegasus Dwarf

• NGC 6822   2 Mly

• IC 1613

• Phoenix Dwarf

3 Mly

• Cetus Dwarf

• Aquarius Dwarf   4 Mly

• WLM

• SagDIG

Mly = million light-years

20

artist illustration of extrasolar planets

Extrasolar Planets

Scientists have studied the planets in our solar system for years. But better telescopes have allowed them to search for planets outside our solar system. Scientists have found about 500 extrasolar planets so far in the Milky Way. One of the most exciting is called Gliese (GLEE-zuh) 581g. This extrasolar planet is very similar to Earth. Does it hold life? No one knows ... yet!

In 2010 scientists discovered the first planet outside the Milky Way. Some believe this proves that many planets orbit inside other galaxies too.

Chapter 4

Studying Galaxies

Most galaxies are too far away for us to see without help. Scientists rely on the latest technologies to study galaxies.

In 1990 NASA launched the Hubble Space Telescope. It orbits about 380 miles (612 km) above Earth. Scientists use computers to tell the telescope which way to point. Hubble uses mirrors to reflect, collect, and focus light. A computer on board records what it sees and sends the information back to Earth.

This telescope is so powerful that it can see light from galaxies billions of light-years away. In 2001 Hubble saw star explosions called supernovas in distant galaxies. Hubble has also allowed scientists to see galaxies crash together. Since 1990 astronauts have repaired and improved the telescope several times. They expect it to work until 2014.

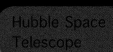

Hubble Space Telescope

James Webb Space Telescope

NASA's James Webb Space Telescope will replace Hubble in 2014. This telescope will focus on even more distant areas of the universe.

It takes a long time for light to travel through the incredible distances in space. Say it takes 10 million light-years for light leaving a galaxy to reach the "eye" of a telescope. The telescope is not seeing today's light. It is seeing light from 10 million years ago. The telescope can look back in time.

Hubble can see back to about 800 million years after the big bang. These images show a teenage universe. James Webb should be able to look back to about 200 million years after the big bang. These images will be like baby pictures. Scientists hope the pictures will increase their understanding of galaxy formation.

James Webb Telescope

Spitzer Space Telescope

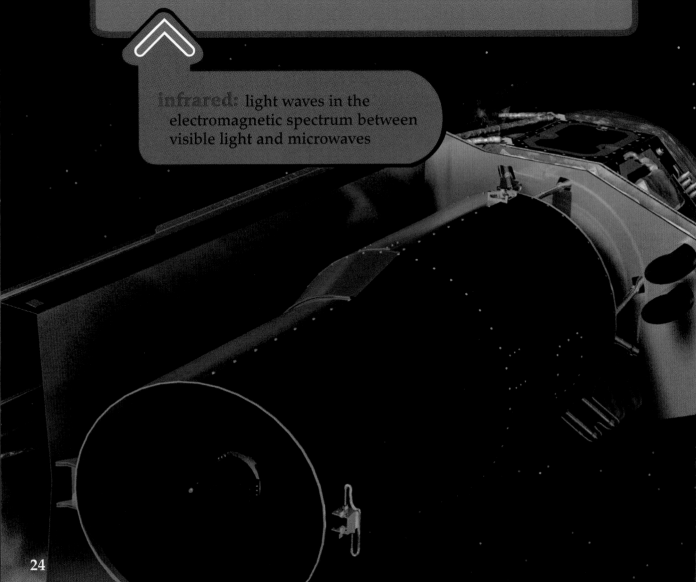

The Spitzer Space Telescope (SST) was sent into orbit in 2003. The SST is an infrared telescope. Infrared light is invisible to our eyes. But this telescope can measure it. Stars, gas, and dust in galaxies give off infrared light. Astronomers use SST to see where new stars are being born in the Milky Way.

infrared: light waves in the electromagnetic spectrum between visible light and microwaves

Space Telescopes

Telescope	Goal	Orbit	Named for
Hubble Space Telescope	to determine the age of the universe	353 miles (568 km) above Earth	Edwin Hubble discovered that Andromeda was a galaxy outside the Milky Way.
James Webb Space Telescope	to discover how galaxies formed	1 million miles (1.6 million km) above Earth	James Webb ran NASA during the first moon landing.
Spitzer Space Telescope	to collect infrared light to find stars	Follows behind Earth as it orbits the Sun	Lyman Spitzer Jr. was a famous scientist and the first to suggest the idea of a space telescope.

AMS-2

Most of our knowledge about galaxies has come from studying light. But scientists think tiny particles in space may also provide information.

The Alpha Magnetic Spectrometer-2 (AMS-2) uses a large magnet to collect space particles. Some scientists think that dark matter creates charged particles. If the AMS-2 picks up these particles, they might be able to measure dark matter.

The AMS-2 was launched in 2011. It weighs 18,739 pounds (8,500 kilograms). It stands 13 feet (4 meters) tall and is 15 feet (5 m) wide. This machine is docked at the *International Space Station.* Scientists hope the AMS-2 will help them learn what makes up the invisible mass in our universe.

particle: a tiny piece of something

charged: an amount of electricity running through something

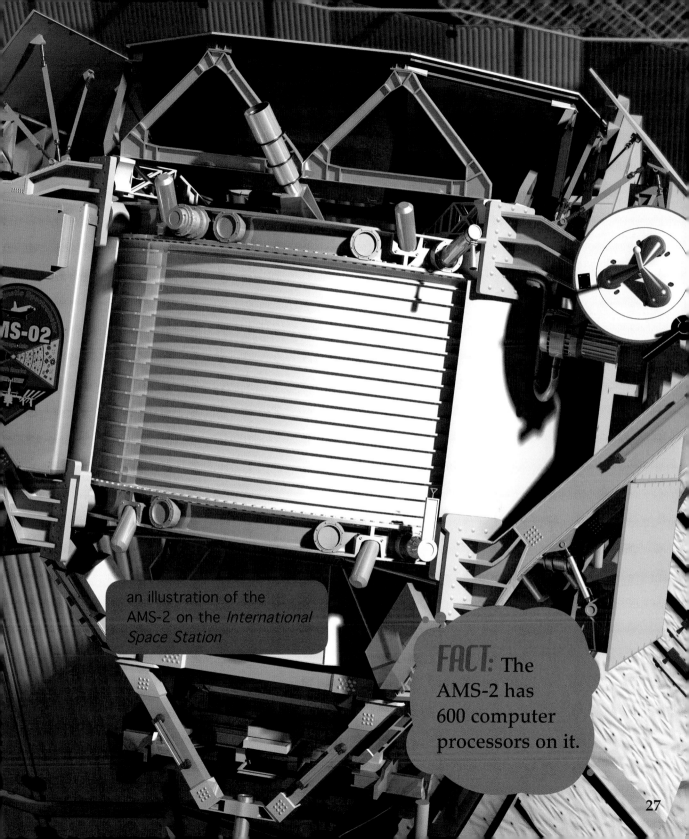

an illustration of the AMS-2 on the *International Space Station*

FACT: The AMS-2 has 600 computer processors on it.

Answering Questions

From the beginning of time, humans have wondered about space. How do galaxies form? What happens when they collide? Is there life in other galaxies?

With new knowledge, scientists continue to expand our understanding of the universe. But as one question is solved, others pop up. Who knows what scientists might learn about our galaxy and those around us?

galaxy M82

Glossary

charge (CHARJ)—an amount of electricity running through something

dwarf galaxy (DWORF GAL-uhk-see)—a small galaxy with only a few billion stars

gravity (GRAV-uh-tee)—a force that pulls objects together; gravity increases as the mass of objects increases or as objects get closer

infrared (in-fruh-RED)—light waves in the electromagnetic spectrum between visible light and microwaves

light-year (LITE-yihr)—a unit for measuring distance in space; a light-year is the distance that light travels in one year

magnify (MAG-nih-fye)—to make something look larger than it really is

mass (MASS)—the amount of material in an object

matter (MAT-ur)—anything that has weight and takes up space

orbit (OR-bit)—the path an object follows as it goes around a dwarf planet, galaxy, planet, or star

particle (PAR-tuh-kuhl)—a tiny piece of something

theory (THEE-ur-ee)—an idea that explains something that is unknown

Read More

Elish, Dan. *Galaxies*. Kaleidoscope. New York: Marshall Cavendish Benchmark, 2007.

Jefferis, David. *Galaxies: Immense Star Islands*. Exploring Our Solar System. New York: Crabtree Publishing Co., 2009.

Trammel, Howard K. *Galaxies*. A True Book. New York: Children's Press, 2010.

Internet Sites

FactHound offers a safe, fun way to find Internet sites related to this book. All of the sites on FactHound have been researched by our staff.

Here's all you do:

Visit *www.facthound.com*

Type in this code: 9781429660020

Super-cool stuff!

Check out projects, games and lots more at
www.capstonekids.com

Index

DATE DUE

DE 2 2 '11		
JA 1 0 '12		
FE 1 4 '12		
MY 2 7 '12		
CL 1 7 AV		
NO 2 2 '16		
JA 1 2 '17		
GAYLORD		PRINTED IN U.S.A.